THE ART OF
PRESSED
LEAVES

JENNIE ASHMORE

THE ART OF
PRESSED
LEAVES

NEW IDEAS IN
PRESSED LEAVES
AND FLOWERS

BATSFORD

First published in the United Kingdom in 2024 by Batsford
43 Great Ormond Street
London WC1N 3HZ
An imprint of B. T. Batsford Holdings Ltd

ISBN 9781849947770

A CIP catalogue record for this book is available from the British Library.

10 9 8 7 6 5 4 3 2 1
30 29 28 27 26 25 24

Reproduction by Toppan Leefung Ltd, China
Printed and bound by Rival Colour Ltd, UK

This book can be ordered direct from the publisher at www.batsford.com
or try your local bookshop.

Disclaimer: Take care to avoid picking rare, protected or poisonous species. Whatever you are picking, don't remove too much at any one time.

Contents

Introduction

In recent years I have become aware of a growing appreciation of the natural world in our society. I have always loved nature, but now many people are retreating into it.

Many artists spend hours collecting natural material, such as twigs, stones, leaves, soil and clay, for use in their artworks. Some people use willow for basketmaking, others make inks, paints and dyes from plants, or paper and books from natural fibres.

There has also been an upsurge of authors writing about their journeys into the wild, exploring the countryside and recording what they see. I believe this is linked with our knowledge of climate change, a general loss of biodiversity and the destruction of many habitats.

Accompanying this has been a growing interest in re-wilding, in our back gardens and beyond, with people growing more wildflowers, leaving grass uncut, planting trees and creating useful habitats for plants and animals.

LEFT *Kirklea Garden, Auchencairn* (2017). 30 x 30 cm (12 x 12 in)

My own work has developed somewhat in the last few years. I incorporate a variety of techniques into my pieces, no longer relying on cut squares to create patchwork designs. Many of these techniques, like collagraphing, monoprinting and rubbing, will be covered in the following pages. Of course, much of this is reliant on collecting large quantities of leaves for pressing and, as I have recently moved back to Wales, I can now appreciate beautiful new landscapes which inspire my work.

In this book, I have included information on creating 'leafworks' (artworks made using pressed leaves and flowers) using geometric designs. This can be a good starting point. I also illustrate how to develop a freer approach, incorporating rubbings and simple printmaking with more information on colour, shape and making inks from natural materials.

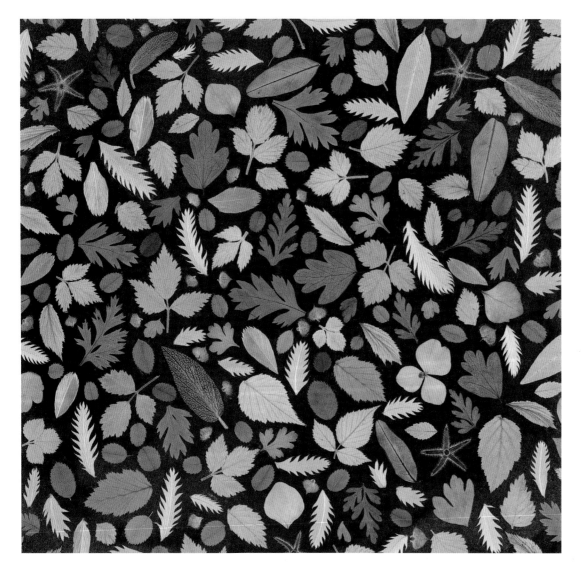

LEFT A variety of small grey leaves on a contrasting black background.

RIGHT *Fern Landscape* (2021). 40 x 40 cm (16 x 16 in)

ESSENTIALS

Collecting

Almost every time I go for a walk, I am on the lookout for suitable leaves and flowers to collect. I am very familiar with my locality, and I particularly look forward to the early spring to see how plants have fared over the winter. There is always the risk that some may have been lost due to environmental damage, or they may have just disappeared.

Some plants keep growing throughout the winter, some even flowering unexpectedly, like red campion (*Silene dioica*). The seasons are changing, with trees and plants reported to be flowering up to a month early in some parts of the country.

Suitable leaves and flowers can be found everywhere, from beautiful gardens to woodland and wasteland. It is important to collect material as it appears; it won't always be there, and it is a long year's wait in most cases for the plants to appear again. I have to remember to visit certain places at the right time of year to collect what I need, which is why record-keeping is important; I always note where and when I have collected certain flowers or leaves.

It takes a while to process the material and arrange it in the pressing book, so it's important not to collect too much at once. Keep flowers separate from leaves – in a small container or different bags – as the flowers can be damaged by the heavier leaf material.

Not everything is suitable for pressing, so I always avoid conifers, most evergreen shrubs and complicated flowers. Always be on the lookout for leaves with insect damage or unusual spots as these can have very interesting textures and colours.

BELOW LEFT Tulips press very well if you separate the petals; they have a lovely silky quality.

BELOW CENTRE *Ginkgo biloba* leaves in a Welsh arboretum; a beautiful yellow that presses well and keeps its colour.

BELOW RIGHT Japanese Rose (*Rosa rugosa*). The large pink petals found on this very common rose keep their magenta colour very well.

I pick everything when it is dry: wet leaves and flowers do not press well and go mouldy. From time to time, I will find something that is damp, especially during the winter, and this material can be dried between sheets of newspaper, weighed down with something heavy, before moving to the pressing book. It is also possible to dry individual leaves with kitchen paper.

I am careful to pick only very small quantities of wild flowers unless they are very prolific and common, like daisies or buttercups for example. I never collect anything unusual. These days I am more likely to collect small leaves and give the flowers a miss, leaving them to the bees and butterflies.

I grow a number of wild plants in my garden, and this makes collecting much easier, for example selfheal (*Prunella vulgaris*), silverweed (*Potentilla anserina*), bedstraws, daisies (*Bellis perennis*), ferns and sweet woodruff (*Galium odoratum*).

It is important to ask permission if collecting from a special garden or park. Gardeners are usually only too happy to share some of their treasures, and I find this is a good way of finding new and interesting material. If I collect from a private garden, I usually give the owner a small finished leafwork or perhaps some cards as a thank you. Public gardens, arboretums and parks are a great way of finding special plants and new discoveries.

I have far too many pressed leaves in store, but I continue to stockpile my favourites! However, I do find that some of the older material becomes brittle and therefore not suitable for use, and from time to time I have a big clear-out.

ABOVE LEFT Hydrangea flowers and autumn reds, collected and waiting to be pressed.

LEFT A bag of autumn leaves waiting to be sorted and pressed.

RIGHT Wet maple leaves on a layer of newspaper, ready for another layer to be placed on the top, weighed down with a couple of heavy books.

LEFT Beech leaves showing a lovely variety of colour.

TOP Leaves showing interesting lines made by the leaf miner beetle.

ABOVE Beautiful flowers of potentilla 'Miss Wilmot' showing their very useful heart-shaped petals.

TOP RIGHT Willow leaves showing good texture.

RIGHT Dandelion sepals after the seeds have been removed.

Pressing

Make sure everything collected is dry, and cut woody stems from leaves if necessary. Large leaves can be cut into pieces to fit in the pressing book.

I use old large telephone books to press leaves and flowers in. Any large-sized old book will do, even a catalogue or magazine.

Place the material between two sheets of photocopying paper, starting at the back of the book. Allow at least 2 cm (1½ in) between each layer. There is no need to fill the book in one go, just add leaves and flowers gradually as necessary.

Small things, like parts of flowers or complicated seed heads like honesty, take a while to process. This involves separating the small flowers from the stems, as in elderflowers, a lovely summer crop. The heads of elderflowers are composed of hundreds of tiny white flowers, which are beautiful to use when pressed. It takes a while to divide the individual flowers from the stems. Keep this in mind when out collecting. Try not to bring home a huge bag of elderflowers as you will find it takes too long to deal with them all. Of course, you can always make elderflower wine instead!

The pressing book has to be weighed down with something heavy, with other books or heavy weights of some kind, whether it is full or not. This has to be left somewhere dry and undisturbed. If weight is not applied, the leaves will not press flat, and the material will be wasted. The pressing book has to be left for a couple of months; however, it is possible to carefully check how things are going.

ABOVE LEFT Summer garden petals and flower heads, including daisies and hardy geraniums, in between the pages of a pressing book laid on a sheet of photocopying paper, with another sheet to be placed on top.

LEFT Telephone books weighed down with two heavy books, showing layers of pressed material, clearly labelled, between photocopying paper.

RIGHT Autumn hawthorn leaves in pressing book.

I always label everything I collect with the name of the plant and when and where the material was found. With a small collection, it is easy to remember where flowers and leaves were found, but I collect a lot of material during a year and I have to label everything. It saves a lot of time searching for things.

Another way to itemize everything is to press all of the same plant in one book, ash leaves for example. I also differentiate between wild and garden material as this makes everything easier to find.

When ready, I keep the pressed leaves in the books to store them, and I usually have up to eighty books full of material ready to use. I collect far too much and eventually I have to store some leaves and flowers in plastic wallets in drawers.

ABOVE Elderflowers being prepared for pressing by separating the individual flowers.

LEFT Elderflowers being prepared for pressing by separating the individual flowers.

20

RIGHT Parts of geranium flowers.

BELOW Rosebay willow flowers after they have been detached from the main stem to make pressing easier.

Basic materials

Working with pressed leaves and flowers requires very little equipment, but it is a good idea to give yourself a space to work in and to store your dried material where it will be kept dry and undisturbed. It is easier to work on smaller pieces of card or paper when you first start exploring making leaf collages. I began by making pieces of work no larger than 15 × 15 cm.

Paper and card

I always use a good quality watercolour paper of medium weight, not too heavily textured, or mountboard, which comes in different colours and can be cut to size as necessary.

You can try other cards and papers, just remember not to use thin paper as it will warp when the adhesive is applied. Thin paper can be glued to a piece of card and then used as a background for a leaf collage. All kinds of paper and card are available and it is always possible to make your own paper, adding flowers and leaves to the mix, which can result in some very beautiful effects.

Pressed leaves can also be applied to other surfaces like wood or plaster. Using a glue stick, it is possible to apply pressed leaves to decorate wooden boxes, furniture and even a wooden floor. The leaves would have to be given several coats of varnish to protect the design. This traditional technique is called decoupage, and in the past it has been used to decorate furniture with paper cut-outs or pictures. I think this is an area that could be explored using pressed leaves and flowers.

Adhesives

Copydex is a rubber-based adhesive and is the only adhesive I use for pressed leaves and flowers. Always squeeze out a small amount onto a piece of card or a tile, or something similar. I apply the adhesive to the pressed piece with a sharpened matchstick which ensures only a small amount is used – too much glue can spread onto the paper. It can be removed when dry, but there is a risk of damaging the dried material. Small bits of unwanted adhesive can also be removed using the matchstick or just by carefully rubbing. When applying adhesive to delicate petals and other thin material, use tiny dots of the glue.

ABOVE Pressed ferns
on different papers and
coloured card.

ABOVE LEFT Handmade
paper

LEFT Applying copydex
adhesive to a cut square
using a matchstick.

COLOUR

Using painted backgrounds

Fresh leaves and flowers, in the garden or the wild, are mostly bright and colourful. This changes during the pressing process; the brightness often fades, with a few exceptions, and many leaves and flowers change to a dull fawn or brown – not very exciting. This happens particularly with most shades of green, a colour seen everywhere.

It is always possible to work around this by creatively using tone and texture, alongside colour. For example, when embarking on a geometric piece using cut squares, always look out for creating contrast in the design, by using dark and light shades together, or by putting certain colours together, such as red and green. You can also use texture to add contrast to the work, such as the spots, blotches and stripes found on some leaves.

After many years of working only geometrically, I moved onto a freer style that uses small bits and pieces placed in lines on white paper. From there, I developed more colourful backgrounds using coloured card or painted with gouache or watercolour paint on a good watercolour paper.

I realised I could re-create geometric designs in a simpler way, by painting horizontal or vertical stripes and using this background to place the small bits and pieces. The coloured background supports the dried pressed material, which may fade over time, but the paint will not fade.

Red stripes

I painted vertical stripes of colour using a wash of gouache paint and lots of water, allowing the first layer to dry before painting the darker shades. When dry, I used an assortment of small, pressed material to decorate the stripes. The design is governed by the width of the stripes, and it is important to have plenty of bits and pieces to choose from.

Green horizontal stripes

In a similar way, these painted green horizontal stripes immediately lend themselves to a landscape design.

Blue vertical and horizontal stripes

Using ultramarine gouache and water, I painted stripes both up and across, creating a framework in which to apply small pieces of pressed material. I placed the larger darker shapes first (nettles/borage/ferns) and then composed the design, balancing the colours with light shades on dark and dark shades on light.

I used plenty of potentilla red hearts to tie the design together and provide dots of vibrant colour set against the blue background.

Two colour design

By using vertical and horizontal stripes of blue and yellow, I was able to create a symmetrical design with space for pressed material to be placed.

Certain colours look very good on black card, such as red or silver. It is possible to use all shades of coloured card, but I prefer to use painted backgrounds as I feel they are more subtle and painterly. When the finished piece is framed and hung on the wall, fading will continue as the pressed material will now be exposed to the light. I always hang my work out of direct sunlight, but it is possible to expose a picture to bright sunshine and see how the colours change. These changes can be very beautiful! Quite often, lovely things can happen that are unintentional and accidental. I see this as part of the creative process.

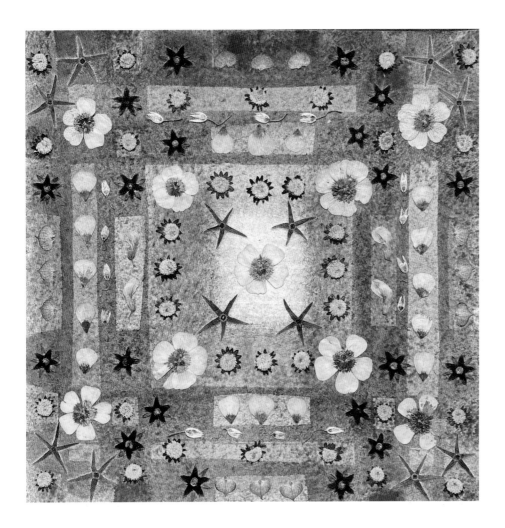

LEFT These small pieces of work do require a lot of dried material to complete the design.

RIGHT A large, finished design.

Yellow

Yellow can be surprisingly good because a lot of yellow flowers keep their colour really well, particularly buttercups (*Ranunculus acris*), primroses (*Primula vulgaris*), celandines (*Ranunculus ficaria*) and violas. Yellow leaves are a bit more unreliable. In the autumn there are many shades of yellows to be found, such as runner bean leaves, elm (*Ulmus procera*) and many members of the Acer family, but when pressed, all these leaves will turn orange or brown.

RIGHT A variety of greens.

FAR RIGHT Left to right: top row – willow, primrose, lime, celandines; second row – Jack-by-the-hedge, cow parsley, angelica; third row – buttercups, hawthorn, blackthorn, brassica flowers; fourth row – willow, hawthorn, climbing hydrangea, willow, pansy

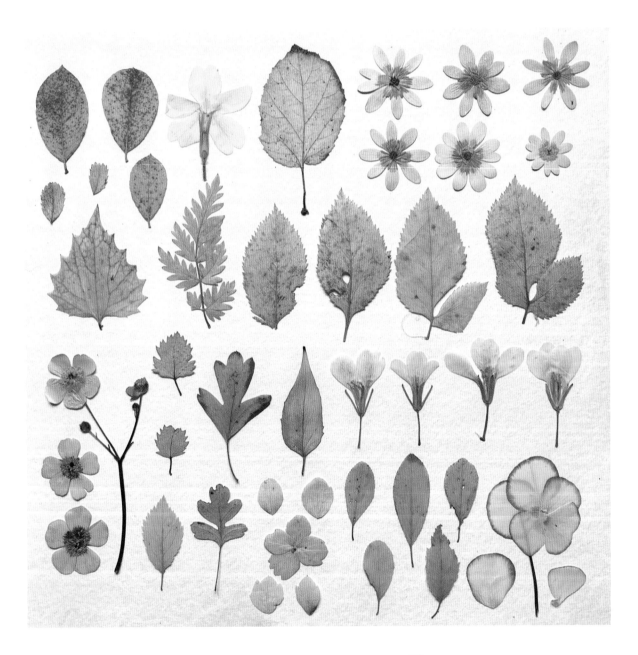

LEFT Left to right: top row – rowan, montbretia, cercis, Welsh poppy; second row – beech, herb Robert, cercis, hardy geranium; third row – hardy geranium, grapevine, willow herb; fourth row – blueberry, Virginia creeper; fifth row – hawthorn, cotinus, potentilla, shining cranesbill, Virginia creeper

Green

As I have previously mentioned, green is by far the most elusive colour when pressed. It can be quite disappointing to press bright spring greens and find they have all changed to ochre, beige or brown. These more subtle colours can also be beautiful, depending on how the pressed material is used.

Nettles (*Urtica dioica*) have a wonderful dark bottle-green that keep their colour when pressed well. They are found everywhere but you need to wear gloves when collecting! Interestingly, the leaves lose their sting when pressed. Other greens will fade but the results can still be very beautiful.

Reds and oranges

These colours are found in profusion in autumn. Particularly good are the Virginia creeper (*Parthenocissus quinquefolia*) and grape vines. Rowan (*Sorbus acuparia*), shining cranesbill (*Geranium lucidum*), herb robert (*Geranium robertianum*) all have lovely red leaves and can be easily found at the end of the summer. Yellow Welsh poppies (*Meconopsis cambrica*) become a beautiful orange when the petals are pressed.

Arboretums and private gardens are good places to find all manner of red leaves in the autumn.

Silver, grey and white

I love using silver and grey foliage, usually placing the design on a black background. The colour is fairly constant, and the silvery effects do not change. White can be more elusive as many white flowers, such as rose petals, become brown when pressed.

There are only one or two very good silver/whites to be found in the British wild, notably Silverweed, one of my essentials. This plant grows happily in all kinds of habitats, from sandy beaches to gardens and field margins. The leaves have an interesting shape and I use them singly or the top three leaves as one piece. The highlight is the beautiful silver underside.

Wild raspberry (*Rubus idaeus*) grows everywhere, in the wild or the kitchen garden. Its leaf has a large grey underside that is very useful for cutting squares. I like to use them in early spring as they have a nice decorative shape.

Lichens are often grey or grey/green, and this plant can be found in woodland growing on tree branches. Please only collect lichen when it has fallen to the ground after being blown from the trees, and never pull the lichen off the tree itself.

Wild garlic flowers (*Allium ursinum*), cow parsley (Anthricus sylvestris) and daisies (*Bellis perenne*) all keep their shades of white well and are perfect to use in all kinds of designs.

Other garden plants, including the beautiful alpine lady's mantle (*Alchemilla alpina*), oleaster (*Eleagnus augustifolia*), *cineraria* 'Silver Dust' and members of the artemisia family all have very good silvery foliage and are easy to press.

A superb white flower is to be found on *ammi majus*, a lovely garden umbrella-like plant, much used in flower arranging.

BELOW Left to right: top row – ammi, lichen, cow parsley, silverweed; second row – meadowsweet, alpine alchemilla, wild garlic, sage leaves; third row – daisies, alpine alchemilla, senecio, blackberry, potentilla, rue

LEFT Left to right: top row – poppies; second row – Tibetan poppy, hardy geranium, bluebell, heuchera; third row – iris, hydrangea

Blue and purple

It is difficult to find any true-blue flowers that will keep their colour when pressed. The Himalayan poppy (*Meconopsis betonicifolia*) is worth trying because it has a beautiful turquoise blue, but sometimes it will keep its colour well, and sometimes not.

Heuchera (*Heuchera micrantha*) are excellent for shades of purple, found on the underside of their leaves.

Poppies (*Papaver* spp.) of all kinds are very good for purples and dark reds.

Hardy geraniums sport purple, magenta and pink petals. Garden irises also display dark and rich purples. Gardens are usually the best place to find these colours as there are not many to be found in the wild.

GEOMETRY

Squares

The square has to be for me, the best shape to work with when cutting pressed leaves with a template. It is possible to build hundreds of different designs using this simple shape. The small square is also so useful as it fits well on to most of the leaves that I find, giving an unlimited variety of colours and textures to work with. It is possible to cut at least a dozen squares from some large sycamore leaves. The example I give here, *Askham Woods, Cumbria,* is quite a complex design but a smaller version of this design would be a good way to start using simple geometric patterns.

I collected leaves regularly and pressed them in my telephone books, recording what I had found. The books were left until the material was completely dry and flat, like pieces of paper.

When collecting I always make sure that I gather a variety of colours, dark and light greens, yellows, reds and oranges, which will provide me with a good palette of colours to work with. I love the contrasts between the lighter and darker shades.

I chose a large piece of thick white card, 100 × 100 cm (39 × 39 in), and as always with this geometric style, I started by marking the centre of the card and drawing a cross. The first square was placed on the exact centre and from there I could plan my design.

RIGHT Cutting squares using a metal template and a Stanley knife. I like to cut a good number of pieces for a large-sized work like this.

I use a template to cut my squares. This can be made of card, plastic or metal. I chose to use a metal template of 2.5 cm (1 in) in size. This small square gives me hundreds of design possibilities and up to now I have not wanted to try other sizes or shapes. The small square works so well and is an ideal size for cutting squares from leaves.

I use a Stanley knife to cut the squares out. I place the template on the pressed leaf and carefully cut round it; a scalpel or craft knife would also be suitable. The blade needs to be sharp.

My first square was placed in the exact centre of the cross, and from there my design slowly developed, piece by piece, arranging the squares in a symmetrical design, and checking to see how it worked visually as I went along by looking at the work from a distance.

I have a rough idea of the overall pattern, but it often works out very differently. It all depends on the leaves and the colours I have available.

The squares are attached to the card with Copydex adhesive. I use a long sharpened matchstick to apply small quantities to the back of each square, making sure the whole surface is coated with adhesive, and I then place the square in position and press down firmly.

It was important for me to have enough squares to complete the work. In this case I cut 841 squares, which required lots of pressed leaves to work with. I never plan the design too rigidly; I tend to build the pattern from the centre outwards and see how it goes. I am guided by the leaves and the chosen colours.

It is always possible to make a clear plan before you start, drawing out a pattern on graph paper. Some people would find this easier. One of the problems that can occur when using cut-out squares, whatever the design, is that the edge can become very uneven. This can happen quite often, and I usually take a steel ruler and a sharp Stanley knife and trim the uneven edge carefully, not taking too much away. A certain amount of unevenness is acceptable I think; no one is looking for absolute perfection, which is hard to achieve when using natural materials.

As each section is finished, it is always a good idea to cover what has been done with thin paper and press the squares down with heavy books as this will help the adhesive and paper to bond.

I completed the piece by adding rows of silverweed leaves (*Potentilla anserina*) in a zigzag arrangement, and placed hawthorn leaves (*Crataegus monogyna*) and other small items in the light-coloured squares, which added more colour and texture.

LEFT *Askham Woods, Cumbria.* 100 x 100 cm (39 x 39in). This piece demonstrates the importance of dark and light shades to provide the contrasts needed for this kind of work. If you have no light shades, then watercolour paints could be used instead.

Circles

Quite recently I discovered the circle! After many years of cutting leaves using a square template and creating symmetrical pieces of work, I had an opportunity to change things completely and use the circle as another of my basic shapes. I felt this idea linked well with other things that were going on in the world, with a lot of discussion about climate change and the effect of environmental damage to the Earth.

The idea of the circle representing the Earth was very pleasing to me and I have used the format many times recently. The technique is just as time-consuming as cutting squares as I have to have in front of me hundreds of small pieces of pressed material to choose from. Each shape has to be just right, and it often takes me a while to select the perfect small leaf or flower.

RIGHT Large autumn circle using a variety of small pieces on a black background (2019). 60 x 60 cm (23½ x 23½in)

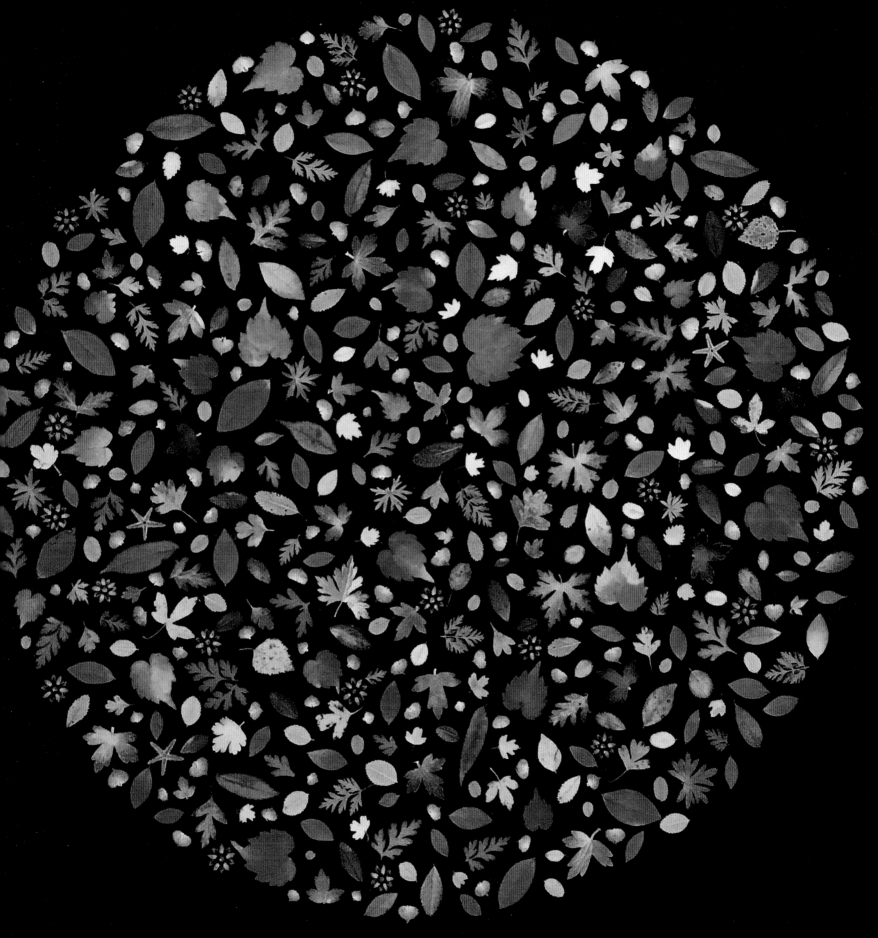

LEFT A small circle showing the white template laid on top of the background and building up the design.

RIGHT Finished piece with template removed. 20 x 20 cm (8 x 8in)

To start with, I cut a circle from a piece of thin card, and put it on one side (this is not used). I use the outer edge of the piece of card left and place this on a suitable piece of mountboard. This gives me an 'empty' circle to work on. This method is better than drawing a circle directly on the board: a drawn line is very visible and impossible to erase when the work is complete as it would damage my design.

I make sure I have enough material to complete the work. I always use very small leaves and petals for these circular designs, and it is surprising how many are needed, even for a small circle. I usually begin anywhere in the circle, and I lay the first pieces down, fixing in place with adhesive when I am happy with the arrangement.

In *Hearts & Borage*, I used borage calyxes, placing them around the edge of the circle with the heart-shaped petals of potentilla. From there, I worked on the central area, placing more borage and hearts and then surrounding these with lots of small foliage.

In a more random arrangement it is important to turn the circle as the design has to be balanced with the material evenly distributed.

I also painted my own watercolour background for some of the Earth series. It provides me with a subtle surface to work on. You can also use coloured mountboard.

ABOVE LEFT *Hearts & Borage*. Building the design from the outer edge.

LEFT Detail of *Hearts & Borage*.

RIGHT *Hearts & Borage* (2020). Finished piece. 40 x 40 cm (16 x 16in)

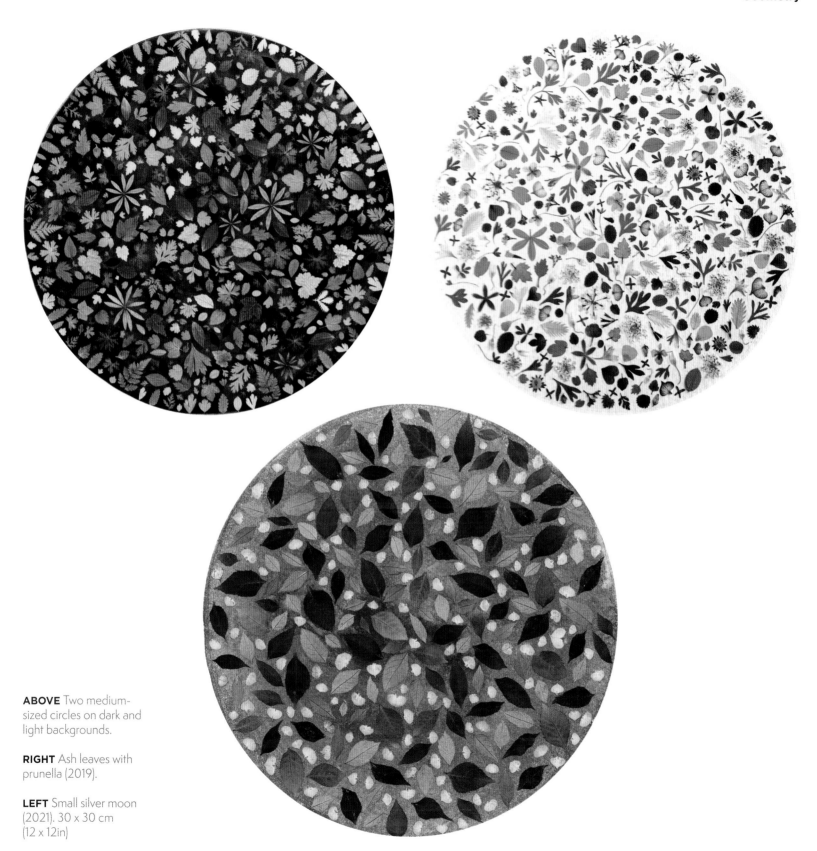

ABOVE Two medium-sized circles on dark and light backgrounds.

RIGHT Ash leaves with prunella (2019).

LEFT Small silver moon (2021). 30 x 30 cm (12 x 12in)

Other Shapes

Different, dynamic shapes can be made by turning the square template 45°. As in patchwork, the designs can get quite complicated, and the possibilities are infinite if you like symmetry.

BELOW Metal template turned 45° to cut out new shape.

RIGHT New shape used to build up a different geometric pattern.

ABOVE Heart shaped cut-out, used as a template for potentilla hearts.

ABOVE RIGHT Heart shaped cut-out with potentilla hearts and ammi flowers.

RIGHT Different cut-out shapes.

It is possible to create new shapes by cutting a template using thick paper. Fold the paper in two and draw one half of the chosen shape. Use scissors to cut the shape out. The centrepiece is discarded and the outside edge acts as the template. Remove the template when all the pressed material is glued down. You can also use metal, plastic, and patchwork templates.

FOLIAGE AND HEDGEROW

Inspiration from the natural world

Foliage has been used throughout history as inspiration for fabric, wallpaper, textiles, embroidery, tilework, illuminated manuscripts and many other decorative art forms. Humans have always liked to bring the beauty and designs of the natural world into their homes.

Leaves are ideal for patternmaking, with a wealth of sizes, shapes, and colours available to work with.

I love using small leaves and arranging a collection from somewhere special, like a particular wood or hedgerow which holds meaning for me.

Collecting and pressing hedgerow material

As already mentioned, I have recently moved back to Wales, where my work with leaf collages began many years ago. Everywhere I look there are intricate hedgerows, individual mature oaks and small native woodlands. The hedgerows contain numerous native species of trees and shrubs, and my walks are now spent looking for new material to add to my collection, which in turn gives me inspiration for new work. I look for small leaves with interesting shapes, textures, and colours. I recommend that you look through your local hedgerows in late summer, when many leaves have started to change colour.

OPPOSITE A piece of very fine antique embroidery with tiny stitching on a delicately woven fabric using leaf and flower shapes.

OPPOSITE BACKGROUND Hawthorn leaves, blossoms and branches are patterned with jasmine in this William Morris 1872 wallpaper.

ABOVE LEFT A pile of hedgerow material with pressing book.

ABOVE Small bits and pieces placed in pressing book.

Using hedgerow material

You may use the material you have collected from your local hedgerows in whichever way inspires you, but this is how I have done so.

I like using a watercolour background, on which I paint stripes both horizontally and vertically, creating 'windows' or spaces in which to place the leaves. Holly leaves can only be collected early in the season from the tops of the stems. The older leaves are impossible to press because they have a very rigid curved shape. The younger leaves are softer and will press flat.

LEFT In this example, I placed small pieces of pressed material along a steel ruler, starting at the bottom edge of the paper with 3 cm (1 in) between each row. The finished collage should be well-balanced and feature lots of different leaf examples.

RIGHT Finished hedgerow leafwork.

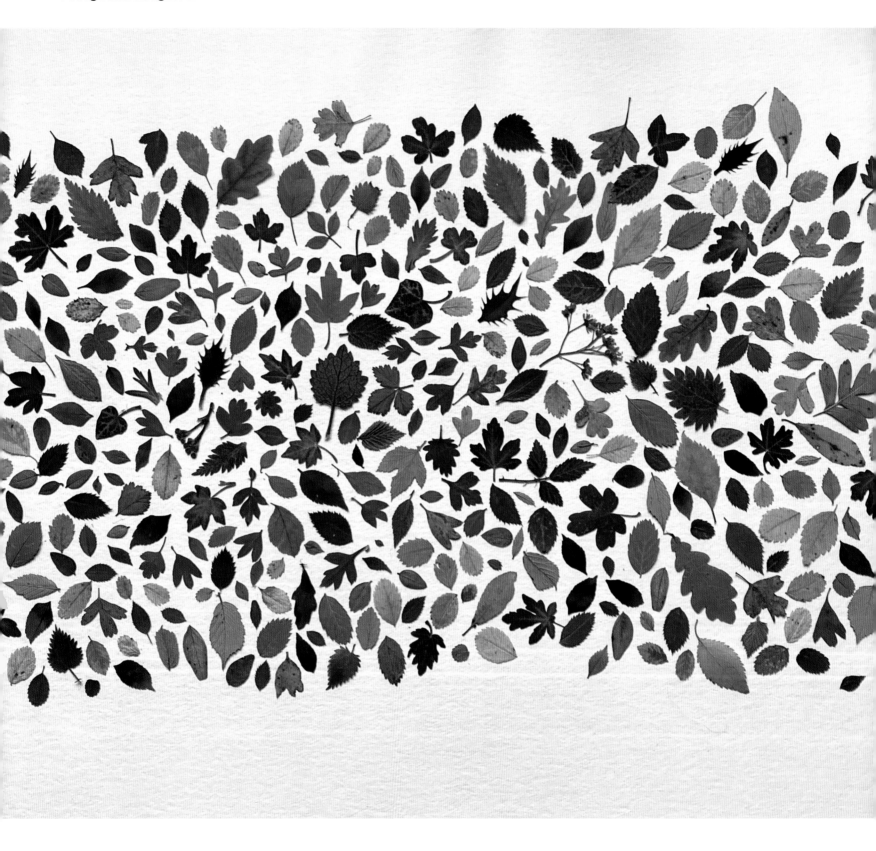

LEFT A freer approach, using hedgerow material, works well. I like the shape it makes on the paper.

RIGHT A more complex design was achieved by painting bands of hawthorn and oak ink. The ink's lovely grainy texture works so well with the pressed leaves.

Hawthorn

Hawthorn is almost my most favourite tree (I am not sure which one is actually my favourite!), with beautifully shaped foliage, a lovely form that is not too huge, and often with gnarled bark and interesting shaped branches. Hawthorns are usually found in hedgerows (they make a perfect hedge) or as single trees, with waves of fabulous white blossom in May.

They are tough, hardy trees, frequently windswept along the coastline where I live, blown almost horizontal with flat tops under which the sheep shelter.

In 2020 a local hawthorn at Kippford won the Woodland Trust's Tree of the Year. I know the tree, which grows on the seashore, and it is a very resilient and beautiful specimen.

The hawthorn's association with fairies is very enticing, and its connection to May Day celebrations, tree worship, religious and pagan symbolism all make the hawthorn an important and intriguing landscape tree.

Hawthorns are also fabulous hosts, in my area, for lichen. Sometimes I come across hawthorns festooned with grey-blue lichen plus the autumn berries. It can be quite a sight.

I collect the leaves in spring when they first emerge. I like their small, complicated shape. In the autumn the leaves change colour, with shades of red, orange and yellow, and I use them frequently in my work.

ABOVE LEFT Hawthorn blossom in spring.

LEFT Hawthorn leaves, midsummer.

RIGHT *Hawthorns.* Pressed leaves with a background of light-coloured squares cut from wild angelica (2020). 20 x 20 cm (8 x 8 in)

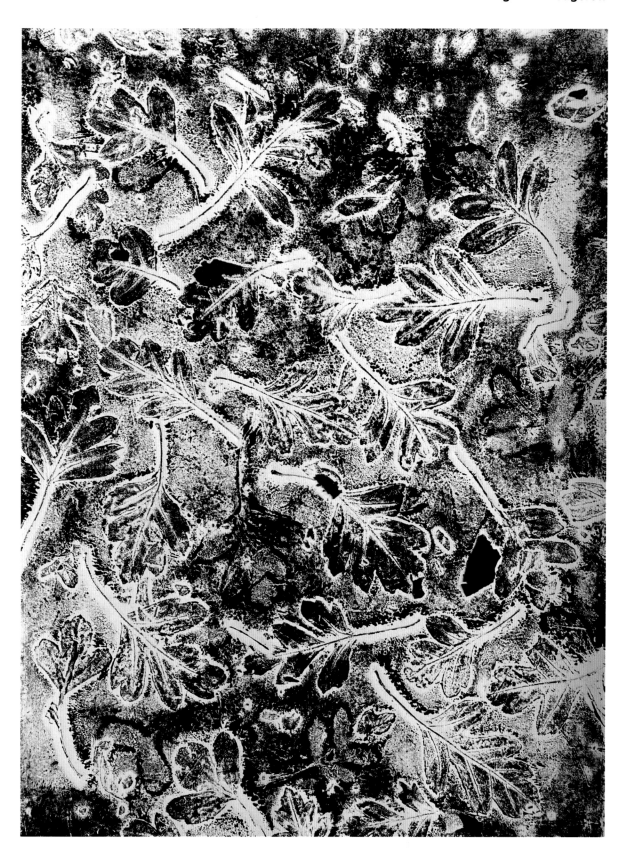

LEFT *Hawthorns II* (2020).
40 x 40 cm (16 x 16 in)

RIGHT Monoprint using
pressed hawthorn leaves.

Making ink from hawthorn leaves

I collect hawthorn leaves and twigs from hedgerows during late summer and autumn; it is possible to use spring leaves too, but the colour won't be as rich, being lighter in shade.

When collecting, handle the small branches carefully as hawthorn carries long sharp thorns, which make it so useful as a stock-proof hedge. Gloves will make gathering leaves much easier.

Remove the leaves from the twigs, put in a bowl and soak for about a week. Very slowly the water becomes orange in colour. I used a small saucepan and heated up the mixture, stirring and being careful not to burn it; the idea is to extract the tannin from the leaves. I also used a small food processor, which chopped the leaves as well, helping to break down the material.

When I was happy with the mix, I strained it into a bowl; at this stage it is possible to test the colour to see how rich – or not – it is. If the mixture is reduced by boiling, the colour definitely intensifies. The other thing I love about working with leaves in this way is the beautiful smell that fills the kitchen!

Adding water to the mixture makes the colour much lighter. The colour of the ink can be modified by adding iron (ferrous sulphate), which can be bought from natural dye suppliers in powder form. Iron 'saddens' the colour, making it a darker shade. Copper sulphate can also be used instead of iron, which has a brightening effect. This also comes in powder form from natural dye suppliers.

BELOW LEFT Preparing hawthorn leaves by soaking in water, with hawthorn twigs and berries.

BELOW Various shades of colours from hawthorn.

RIGHT Hawthorn ink with hawthorn rubbings and pressed leaves (2022). 30 x 40 cm (12 x 16 in)

To preserve the ink, it can be kept in the fridge for a while or decanted into a bottle with the addition of a drop of clove oil (this adds another lovely scent to the ink). If experimenting with lots of different leaves, berries and twigs, label the bottles with the name and date. It is always the case, as one starts trying all manner of natural materials, that things can get a bit chaotic!

Hawthorn berries are prepared in a similar way, chopped up in a food processor or squashed with a rolling pin. The ink from the berries is not red, but another shade of orange.

This process I have outlined is the most basic; it is good to experiment and always try the colours on paper as you go along. When a suitable colour has been achieved, use it up fairly quickly.

Ink-making is a fascinating thing to do and I have enjoyed learning more about the process. The technique marries well with pressed leaves, and I am now experimenting with new ideas for my work.

An interesting thing I have discovered is that usually I would rarely use orange watercolour paint in my work, but here I found that I love the beautiful orange shade of the hawthorn ink, and this has given recent work a new dimension.

ABOVE LEFT Hawthorn ink mixed with copper, indigo and iron, showing more shades that can be achieved. Photographed by The Old Mill Gallery.

LEFT A tin of hawthorn pigment.

Making ink from acorn caps

This process is slightly different from making hawthorn ink as acorn caps are very hard and need to be broken down to extract the pigment.

1   To do this, place the caps on a table and cover them with a cloth. Using a wooden rolling pin, bash the caps until they are broken up into small pieces.
2   From there, use a small food processor to grind the caps even finer.
3   Simmer the powdery acorn caps for about two hours in enough water to cover. This liquid reduces quickly, so check water levels frequently and add more water as it evaporates. If the ink is too watery, the colour will be less intense.
4   Dip a strip of paper into the ink to test the colour.
5   Use a sieve to filter the ink of particles. I sometimes like the particles, so I don't filter too finely. If you prefer a clear ink, use a coffee filter.
6   As when making hawthorn ink, add 10 drops of gum Arabic and a few drops of clove oil to 60ml of ink, then bottle. The gum Arabic acts as a binder and the clove oil prevents the ink from going mouldy.

These homemade inks can be used alongside water-based paints and basic drawing materials like charcoal and graphite. These inks are not very intense so build layers to create deeper shades. Different papers can also affect the density of the colour.

Any natural ink will be light-sensitive and will fade over time, just like pressed leaves, so keep finished work out of direct sunlight.

LEFT The artist Ed Campbell's studio, with many examples of different inks using plants and other natural materials.

RIGHT A richer shade of ink with rubbings and pressed leaves (2022). 40 x 40 cm (16 x 16 in)

Ash

As many people are now aware, the ash tree is threatened by the fungus known as *Hymenoscyphus fraxineus*, ash dieback.

Ash (*Fraxinus excelsior*) is the third most common tree in the UK and the disease is expected to kill millions in the coming years, making a huge impact on our landscape.

Ash is an important part of the ecosystem, and the loss of these beautiful trees will affect not only humans, but the many species who depend on it as a habitat: lichen, mosses, liverworts, fungi, invertebrates, mammals and birds.

I collect ash tree leaves every year. I like to pick the very small early leaves, and I use these in my work; the shape is particularly pleasing.

I have noticed signs of the disease locally, with lovely mature ash trees looking thin in the crown and with leafless branches. I collect from the smaller hedgerow trees that are trimmed back every year, which encourages the growth of the smaller leaves. I put the leaves in closed plastic bags when collecting, and immediately press them when I get home, which avoids any possibility of spreading the fungus.

LEFT Ash tree showing dieback of top branches.

RIGHT *Ash and Ivy* (2019). 40 x 40 cm (16 x 16 in)

LEFT *Ash World Tree 2*. Finished piece showing the use of silver foil wrappers in the design (2016).

RIGHT Detail.

My first piece of work that highlighted the plight of the ash was in 2016. I used the idea of ash being the World Tree as it is in Norse mythology, where the enchanted tree Yggdrasil marked the centre of the universe around which everything flowed. I chose to illustrate this by using ash stems and leaves, combined with a painted background bordered with striped foil paper collected from biscuit wrappers. For me it became an image slightly reminiscent of medieval manuscripts and quite decorative.

Later in the same year, I created a large piece of work for an exhibition called 'Energise', the criteria being 'an exploration of our evolving relationship with the natural world and our impact on it'. I thought that another leafwork highlighting the ash would be just right and would satisfy the concept of the exhibition.

LEFT *Ash Requiem* (2018).
100 x 100 cm (39 x 39 in)

ABOVE Detail.

Much of the mythology of this tree highlights the importance of its relationship with humans and that, in some ways, the health of these powerful trees can be linked to the health of the human population. The certain death of millions of one of our most iconic trees seems to me to reflect the connection between the natural world, the effects of climate change and habitat loss, and how we seem unable to protect the ash and many other species.

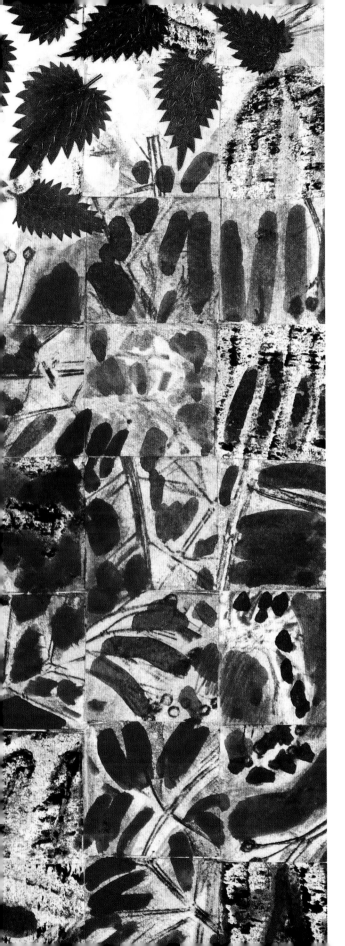

TECHNIQUES

Rubbings

I have always liked using texture in my work, and one very simple technique that requires virtually no equipment is to take a sheet of paper and place it on an interesting surface, like a leaf, a piece of wood with an interesting grain, or something with a strong pattern, such as a book cover or a lacy piece of fabric.

I usually choose leaves with strong ribs and a good shape with an interesting texture. I use a thick piece of graphite; I prefer this to wax crayons or ordinary pencils as I think it brings out more detail in the rubbing. A thick black wax crayon is more useful if taking rubbings outdoors, for example when working with stones, tree bark, wall surfaces or gravestones.

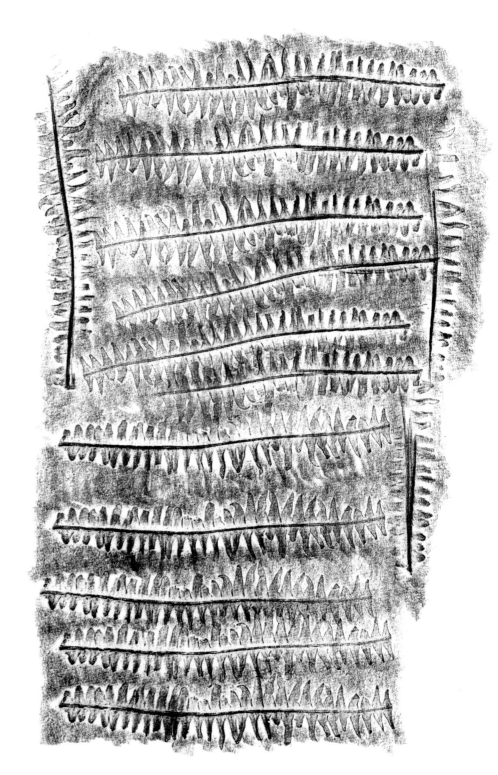

FAR LEFT Hawthorn leaves.

LEFT Lime seed heads.

RIGHT Bracken.

I find there is no need to glue the leaves to the background. It is easy to take a rubbing provided one is very careful not to move the material underneath. I use ordinary photocopying paper, but it is possible to use tissue paper, handmade paper and thin paper of all types. For outdoor rubbings, use a strong paper like rice paper or butchers' paper.

Try to use even pressure throughout, as the harder you press the more detail is shown, and always try to keep the graphite moving in the same direction.

Layers

I like to use a layered approach to this technique. For example, the first layer can be an interesting foliage rubbing; the sheet of paper is then placed on another arrangement of stems or individual leaves, and then I use different shapes for the final layer. It is also possible to work on the finished rubbing with a pencil or even watercolour paint.

Using a template to cut squares from rubbings

To take this process a bit further, I like to cut squares, placing my template over an interesting part of the rubbing. I try to find the most interesting texture or line when I select where to cut the square.

As in my geometrical work, I fix the squares with adhesive to a piece of watercolour paper or card in the same way, starting in the middle and working outwards. I always weigh the finished piece down with a heavy book just to make sure the squares are flat and secured.

During this process take care not to smudge the squares on the edge of the paper – the graphite is soft and gets on your fingers, so mask the edges with pieces of clean paper. If you do get any marks, these can be removed using an ordinary rubber.

LEFT *Senecio cineraria* 'Silver Dust'. Rubbing of pressed leaves using a wax crayon.

RIGHT A larger piece using cut squares of a variety of different rubbings combined with pressed leaves (2022). 40 x 40 cm (16 x 16 in)

Tearing strips of paper

A freer technique I use all the time involves tearing the rubbings into strips. I like to tear the paper instead of cutting with scissors as torn paper has a more interesting, softer edge.

I attach the strips to a larger background of a painted landscape. It is then possible to add more collage material, single pressed leaves, paint or oil pastels to complete the work.

You can also use watercolour and paint over a well-textured rubbing before tearing it up. This adds colour to the textures, which show through well. The combination of these techniques is infinite.

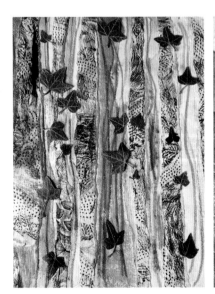 

TOP LEFT Rubbings of pressed leaves torn into strips.

TOP RIGHT Torn strips with pencil and pressed material.

TOP CENTRE LEFT & RIGHT, Experimenting with torn strip of rubbings.

FAR LEFT & LEFT Two finished pieces using torn strips and pressed leaves.

RIGHT Landscape with ash leaves (2021). 50 x 60 cm (20 x 23 ½ in)

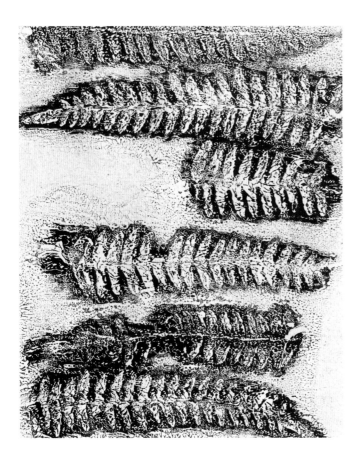

Monoprints

For me, monoprints are a step on from rubbings, resulting in much darker tones and rich blacks. The technique is the simplest form of printmaking and is fairly straightforward to experiment with at home.

Monoprints are unique works, in as much as only one print can be taken, whereas in other types of printmaking, such as linocut, woodcut and etching for example, many prints can be taken from the same block or plate.

Monoprints are easy to do at home as the technique does not require a press (although if you have access to one, then use it!). Prints are created by hand using very basic equipment. First, the water-based ink is rolled out using a rubber roller on a flat, clean plastic or metal sheet. Squeeze out a small amount of ink, being careful not to use too much. Use the roller to spread the ink onto the sheet; when it is right for printing the ink should have a soft, velvety sound.

The most basic form of monoprinting involves drawing directly onto the surface of the ink or making marks of all kinds using different tools, and taking a print by gently pressing down on a sheet of paper placed on top of the ink, with your hand or using a clean roller.

A print can also be made with the back of a wooden spoon, using even pressure throughout. A second print can usually be taken from the inked surface, but the image will be much lighter in tone. More drawing can be done on the paper and it should result in a soft, interesting line.

After applying ink a second time with the roller it is possible to dab textured cloth or paper into the ink, which will leave an imprint in it. A second print can then be taken.

It is also possible, when printing, to lift the corner of the paper to see what is happening underneath without removing the whole sheet. More ink can be applied if necessary.

All kinds of paper can be used, including brown paper, tissue paper, coloured and textured papers, Japanese paper and handmade papers. It is important to experiment with this simple process as it is surprising what can be achieved with such a basic technique.

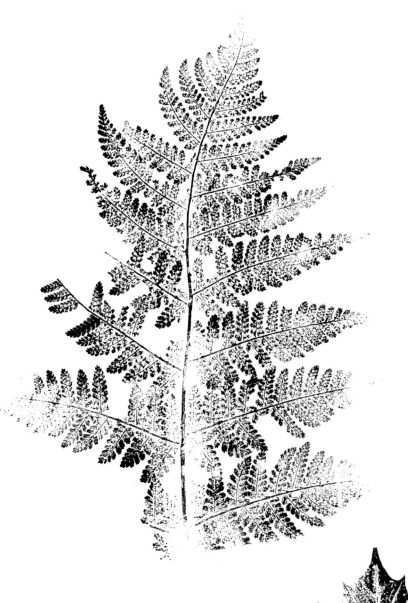

TOP LEFT Bracken leaves.

BOTTOM LEFT Taking a print of bracken.

ABOVE A pressed fern leaf after printing.

ABOVE RIGHT Pressed grasses.

RIGHT Maple leaf.

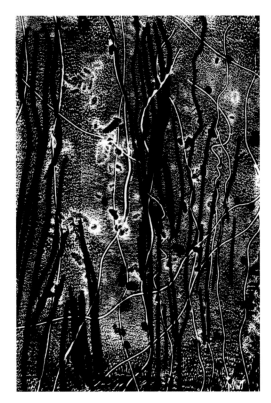  

Using pressed leaves

Roll the plate with ink and place pressed leaves onto the ink; place the paper on top and take a print as before. You could also draw lines on the paper at the same time.

Again, there is a lot of scope with this process. The stencil will show up as the white shape of the leaf. If the leaf is carefully removed from the inked sheet, the shape and texture of the leaf will remain in the ink.

Place another sheet of paper on top and press down very firmly as before. The print will show the details of the leaf. When using leaves, it is best to use well-marked, strong leaves collected in the autumn, for example sycamores and ferns. It is important to experiment and enjoy the process.

To print a leaf directly, ink the leaf with the roller and place it down onto a sheet of paper, cover with another sheet and take a print as before. The leaf will be stuck to the paper so remove it carefully.

LEFT Drawing on the back of a piece of paper as well as pressing firmly with the hand.

CENTRE A print of the inked plate, picking up the white lines drawn in the ink.

RIGHT Hawthorn leaves laid on the inked plate.

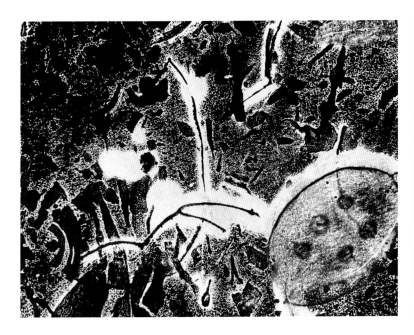

Monoprinting is an altogether different technique from my usual leafworks. It is quite messy for one thing, but I do love the textures that can be achieved. Once the prints have dried, I tear the best ones into strips, and I use some of them on collage work combined with pressed leaves.

Here I have described the most basic forms of printmaking. There are many other results that can be achieved with monoprinting, and there is a wealth of information for ideas on further exploration to be found in books and on the internet.

ABOVE Different textures including honesty seed heads.

ABOVE RIGHT More textures.

RIGHT Hawthorns with white strips of paper placed on the inked plate.

Collagraphs

This is another form of simple printmaking using cardboard and other materials to construct a printing block from which repeat prints can be taken. It is important to try different surfaces and textures, for example fabrics, lace doilies, wallpaper, glue, corrugated cardboard, ribbon, string, sticky tape and anything with an interesting surface.

It is also possible to cut into the surface of the cardboard with a Stanley knife, removing the top layer of the card. This can be marked with holes, scrapes, cuts or any interesting 'damage'.

I use pieces of cardboard cut from packing boxes; however, any card can be used, even a cornflake box. I find a thicker card easier to handle.

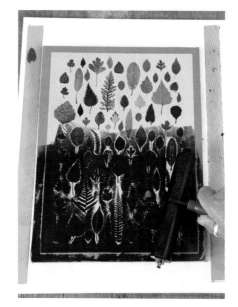

1 For this work I arranged pressed leaves on the card, attaching with adhesive. When I was happy with the design, I painted the surface with two coats of water-based clear wood varnish to protect the design and allow more than one print to be taken.

2 After the varnish was dry, I rolled up the block with water-based printing ink, ensuring the ink was evenly spread. I pressed down on the roller very firmly using two hands and made sure I had applied enough ink to the block.

3 I placed a piece of fairly thick tissue paper over the inked surface and took a print, pressing down firmly and making sure pressure was applied to every corner of the block. It is possible to carefully peel back a corner of the paper to see if enough ink has been applied; if not, more ink can be applied to the block, although it is better to have the right amount in the first place. I always print with my hand and fingers, making sure enough pressure is applied, but not too much in case the paper tears; I like to feel the texture underneath my fingers.

RIGHT Finished print on thick tissue paper (2022). 30 x 40 cm (12 x 16 in)

A second print can be taken without inking the block, it will be much lighter in shade, but can reveal more textures.

This process involves a lot of trial and error, and I am often surprised by the lovely effects and the unexpected results that can occur. The collagraph block is not as permanent as a wood or lino block, but is an experimental process that can be combined with drawing, painting and collage.

As with monoprinting, there is a lot of information about collagraphs to be found on the internet and in books.

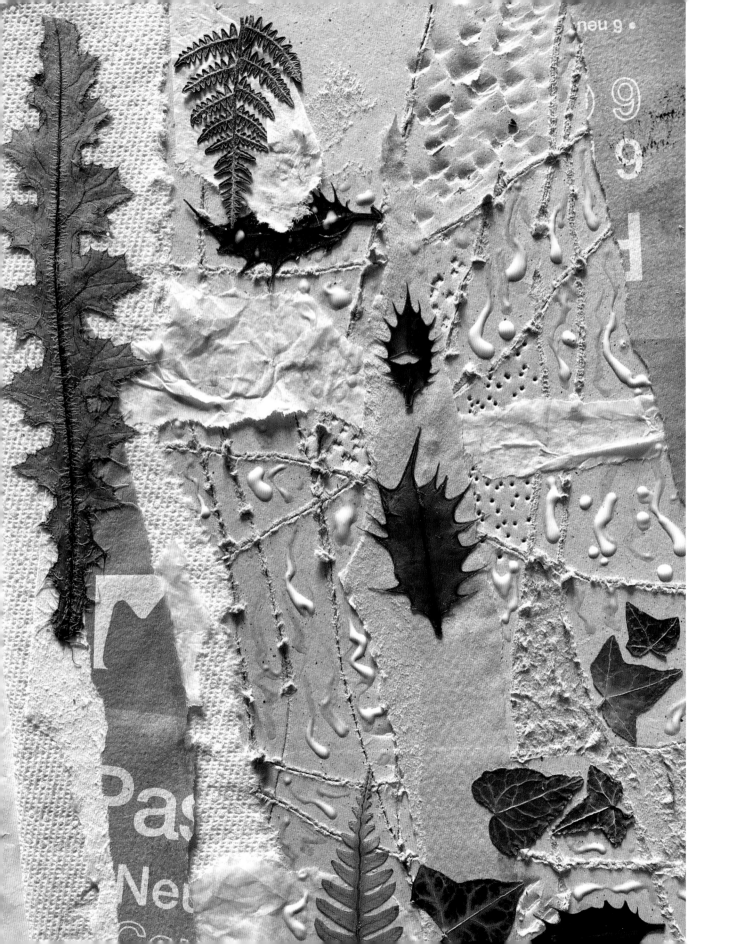

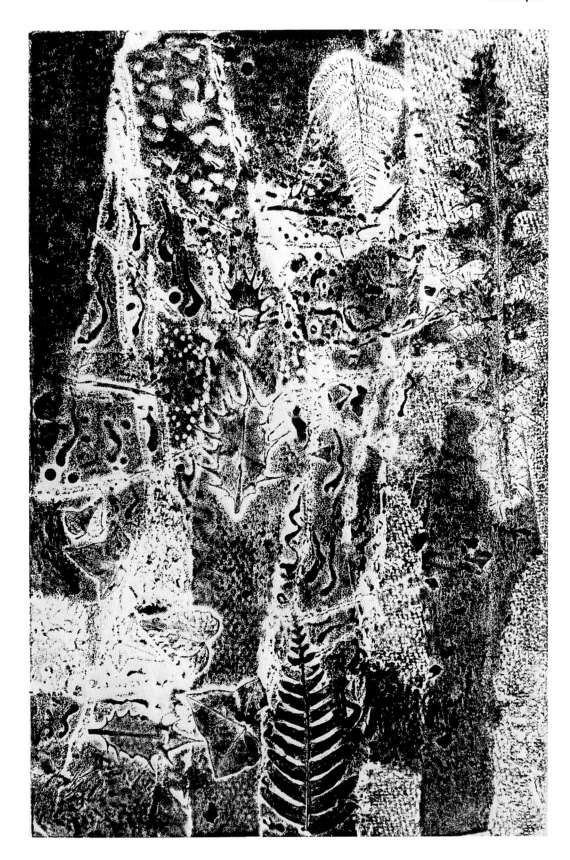

LEFT A finished collagraph block, using pressed leaves, tissue paper and dried PVA glue. Textures are made in the cardboard with a hammer and lines drawn with a bradawl.

RIGHT Finished print clearly showing different textures (2022).
15 x 20 cm (6 x 8 in)

THE SEASONS

Spring

Spring is such a lovely time of year, a season of anticipation and hope, with so much in the natural world to look forward to. Of things waking from a period of quiet, of better weather to come, more light and sunshine.

I am always fascinated when I see the first signs of spring; it is hard to believe how it all works and how the certainty of new growth can strengthen our feelings of optimism, together with the magical, decorative sound of birdsong.

LEFT *Spring Fling.*
40 x 40 cm (16 x 16 in)

Essential plants

I look out for some of the most common plants at this time of year and I return to the same places to find them, which adds to this feeling of reliability.

One of the first flowers to emerge in my part of the world is the **lesser celandine (*Ranunculus ficaria*)**. Another common name for celandine is spring messenger, and its bright, shiny yellow sun-shaped petals open and close during the day according to the light and temperature. The plant is considered invasive in most gardens, and yet they are very beautiful and provide nectar for early insects. I collect only where there are plenty of flowers and in dry sunny weather. It is best to collect the flowers in small batches as they soon close up if left too long before pressing.

Pressing is straightforward: cut off the stem if not required and place the flower head face down onto a sheet of photocopying paper that is in the pressing book. It is important to push down firmly and make sure each petal is pressed flat. These flowers press very well, retaining their beautiful bright yellow colour. It is possible to use both the front and back of the flower heads in a design.

When the flowers are ready to be used, gently lift or prise off the page with a sharp blade. This requires some care as the flowers can get stuck to the paper. Celandines are delightful to use; the flowers brighten up a design and remain strong in colour even after pressing. I have to be careful not to use too many in a leafwork as their colour can be very dominant.

ABOVE LEFT Celandines (*Ranunculus ficaria*).

LEFT Pressed celandine flowers on a green background.

RIGHT Celandines on an ash background with prunella (2020). 20 x 20 cm (8 x 8 in)

Common daisy (*Bellis perennis*) has to be one of the most common flowers. It grows everywhere, preferring short grass. The flower is very pretty; it presses well, keeps its colour and can be used complete or without its petals as it has an interesting centre. I have to remember to collect these flowers. Even though they are very prolific, I find I can easily forget about them.

Sweet woodruff (*Galium odoratum*) is one of my favourite flowers. It is a carpeting woodland plant that likes the shade and will grow happily in the garden, although it can be somewhat invasive. The flowers are white and starry with interesting ruff-like leaves.

I press the stems with the flowers still attached and also detach the leaves from the stem and press separately. The tiny white flowers create little star-like shapes, which I find very useful.

Woodruff is also known for its beautiful scent; the dried leaves retain their perfume and woodruff was once used as a strewing herb.

Other essential spring plants include **wild garlic** (*Allium ursinum*) and other young leaves from trees and bushes.

LEFT Landscape
with a daisy moon (2021).
30 x 40 cm (11 ¾ x 15 ¾ in)

ABOVE RIGHT Common
daisy (*Bellis perennis*).

RIGHT Woodruff
(*Galium odoratum*).

LEFT Scottish flora
(2024). 60 x 60 cm
(23 ½ x 23 ½ in)

ABOVE Bloody cranesbill
(*Geranium sanguineum*).

ABOVE MIDDLE A wild
flower meadow.

ABOVE RIGHT Flowers
and leaves to be pressed.

Summer

Summer is when I turn to my garden, which I have planted with a variety of flowers that I use in my work, including potentillas, hardy geraniums, astrantias, cornflowers (*Centaurea cyanus*), silverweed (*Potentilla anserina*) and poppies (*Papaver* spp.). These are just a few whose summer colours are richer and brighter than most wild flora. Many varieties can be used for pressing and it is best to try the plants you like most and see what happens, as not everything will be suitable when pressed.

I do not collect in the wild quite so much at this time of year, as by summer a lot of leaves have become darker in colour, thicker in texture and much larger. I still keep a look out for small ash and hawthorn leaves, which I find very useful.

Summer is usually a time for holidays, and that can present another opportunity to collect new material and create work as a reminder of the place visited.

I only recommend collecting flora from your own country, as it is not always permitted to import flowers and leaves from abroad because of the risk of spreading plant pathogens.

TOP LEFT Ammi flowers (*Ammi majus*) showing beautiful flat flower heads.

TOP RIGHT Elderflowers being prepared for pressing by separating the individual flowers.

BOTTOM LEFT Individual cornflower petals after pressing.

BOTTOM RIGHT Cornflowers and potentillas before pressing.

Essential plants

Cornflowers (*Centaurea cyanus*)
Elderflowers (*Sambucus racemosa*)
Ammi (*Ammi majus*)

I use the small petals from the cornflower head, the elderflowers and the beautiful pure white flowers of ammi frequently; all three are easy to press.

RIGHT A variety of very small pieces from a summer garden (2020). 30 x 30 cm (12 x 12 in)

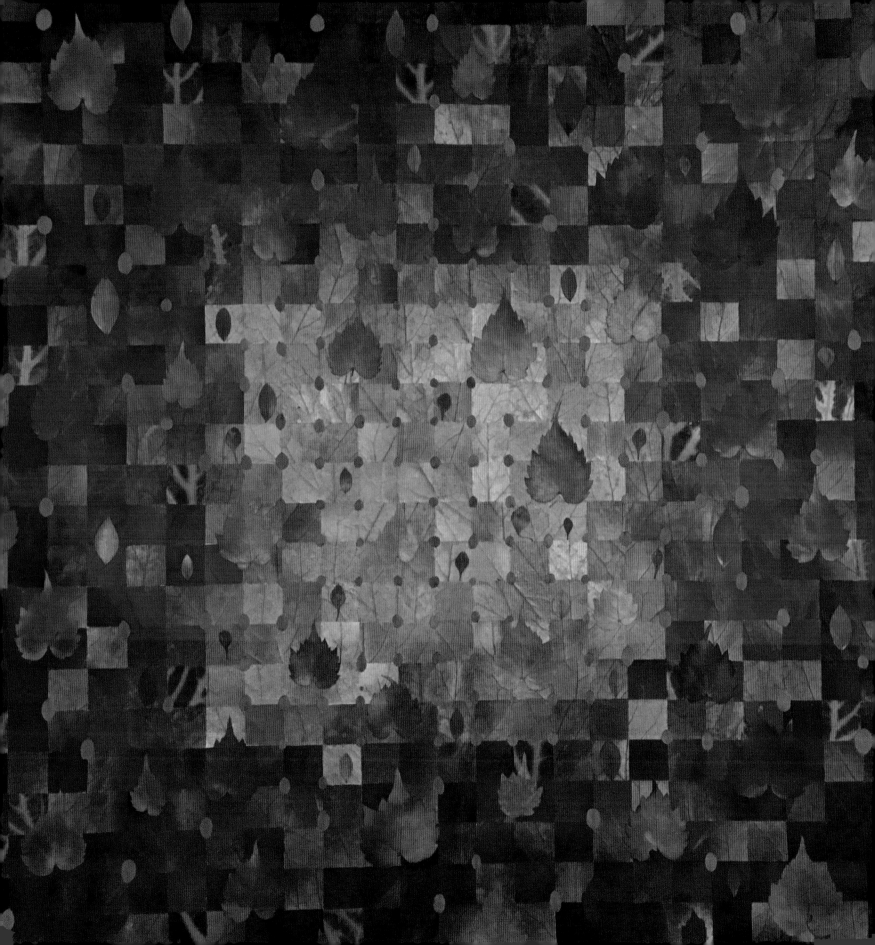

Autumn

I seem to have more autumn photos and pressed leaves than any other season. This special time of year is so significant for the wonderful colour changes that take place in many trees and plants.

I also find that autumn provides relief from the summer, which can be too hot and too overgrown, and I always look forward to the changing season and all the beauty of the falling leaves with their amazing colours. I love the mellowness of this time and I also anticipate the winter and the long period of quiet that comes with it.

Autumn is an important time to go collecting, as the colours change quite quickly and once the cooler temperatures arrive all the leaves will start to fall. This can be a perfect time to visit a botanical garden with collections of unusual shrubs and trees, many exhibiting a lovely variety of reds, yellows and oranges.

When collecting, be aware of wet or damp leaves. They will have to be dried before placing in your pressing books. I do this by laying the leaves out individually on sheets of newspaper, covering with more newspaper, and weighing down with large books or something similar. The weight prevents the leaves from curling up. Wet leaves can also be dried individually with paper towels.

LEFT Finished piece of work, *Autumn* (2019). 100 x 100 cm (39 x 39 in)

LEFT Close-up of *Autumn* showing details of a variety of shades of red and pink with lovely leaf markings.

RIGHT Virginia creeper (*Parthenocissus quinquefolia*).

FAR RIGHT Autumn leaves to be sorted and pressed.

Essential plants

Virginia creeper (*Parthenocissus quinquefolia*) One of my favourites; its large
leaves are bright red and pink with lighter orange shades. The leaves are not too thick
in texture, making the cutting of squares easy. Any very large leaf can be cut up to fit in
the pressing book. Virginia creeper keeps its colour very well.

The acer family (*Acer* spp.) This is a large group of trees and shrubs, some native and many from abroad, and can be found in parks, gardens and in local woods and hedgerows. Acers are grown particularly for their autumn colour and beautiful foliage.

Grapevine (*Vitis* **spp.**) This is another large family of useful and decorative climbing plants. The common grapevine (*Vitis vinifera*) is usually found in greenhouses in the UK, and has the most beautiful leaves, often strikingly patterned in shades of red and yellow. The outdoor garden types are again, like acers, grown for their beautiful autumn colour and their spectacular climbing habit. All vines keep their colour very well.

LEFT Acers.

BELOW Grapevine leaf.

RIGHT Preparing crimson glory vine (*Vitis coignetiae*).

LEFT Finished piece showing a range of autumn shades with the small heart-shaped Virginia creeper leaves (2019). 35 x 35 cm (14 x 14 in)

RIGHT Detail showing a variety of small autumn pieces (2019). 20 x 30 cm (8 x 12 in)

LEFT *Winter* (2021).
20 x 30 cm (8 x 12 in)

RIGHT Frosted winter
leaves.

Winter

I find the season of winter as interesting as the rest of the year, with beautiful light bare stems, neutral tones and evergreens coming into their own. Frost enhances all this and fallen leaves covered in sparkles are magical.

Many plants are still growing in the months of December and January. Small leaves continue to be found on the plants growing in lawns and gardens or roadsides, with many ferns growing beautifully in woodland.

All the broadleaf leaves have usually fallen by this time of year, with one or two exceptions, notably oak and beech, which can linger on for a long while, almost until the following spring, when the new growth bursts through.

Fallen leaves can be collected from the ground; even if they are covered in frost and slightly damaged they can be very interesting. Some may be skeletonized, which are very beautiful, although they are unusual.

I love the neutral colours of winter leaves and they often have interesting textured surfaces, especially the sycamores. After falling from the tree, the leaves lose their green colour completely and become pale beige to white, with the structure of the leaf quite visible, and often with dark spots from tar fungus. There is definitely an antique look about them, which I particularly like.

111

Essential plants

Ferns Our local woods are full of ferns, and in the winter they become very visible, as the foliage is not competing with everything else. Ferns can be almost evergreen and contrast well with the bare branches of the trees. Ferns press very well and can be used in a variety of ways as they are, or used as tree forms in landscape or in monoprinting.

ABOVE LEFT Ferns growing in a wall.

LEFT Woodland fern.

RIGHT *Fern Landscape* (2021). 40 x 40 cm (16 x 16 in)

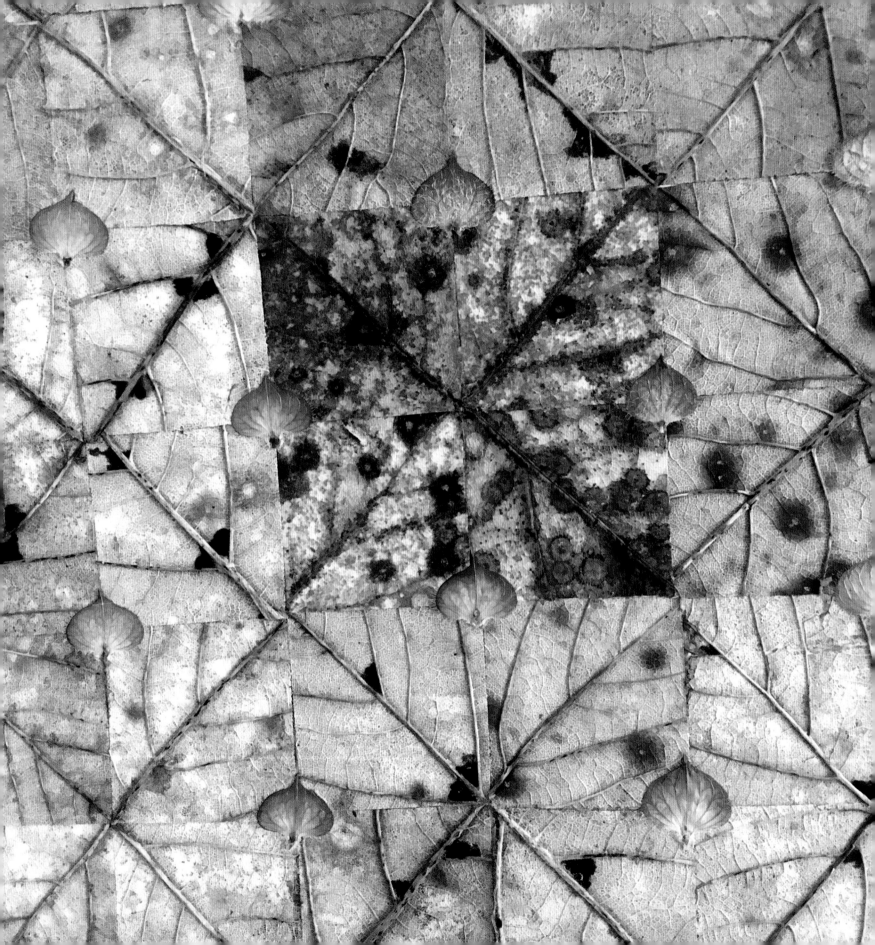

Wood sorrel (*Oxalis acetosella*) This plant has a pretty heart-shaped leaf with tiny white flowers in the spring. Wood sorrel likes the shade and, like ferns, grows happily in woods. In winter the leaves remain in the shelter of the trees and can be collected by taking one or two leaves from each clump. The individual leaves grow in threes and have to be carefully flattened when pressed.

Sycamore (*Acer pseudoplatanus*) I make no apology for highlighting this tree again, which has the very beautiful neutral colours found in the fallen leaves that remain on the woodland floor for weeks, gradually becoming bleached out, giving the antique colour I like so much.

LEFT Bleached sycamore leaves cut on the diagonal to highlight the rib pattern.

RIGHT Wood sorrel (*Oxalis acetosella*).

GALLERY

More leafworks

The following pages include a selection of leafworks created specifically for exhibitions and open studio events during the last seven years, showing my creative development and interests during those years. I have added further contextual information for a few particular pieces: the Galloway Hoard series, the Isle of Coll pieces and Paradise Garden.

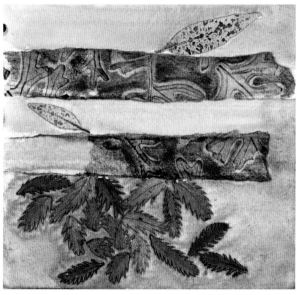

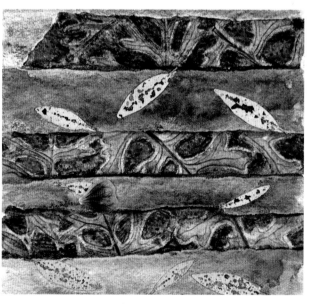

LEFT Small experiments using rubbings, pressed leaves and watercolour paint and oil pastels.

RIGHT Ash leaves with wild angelica (2019). 40 x 40 cm (16 x 16 in)

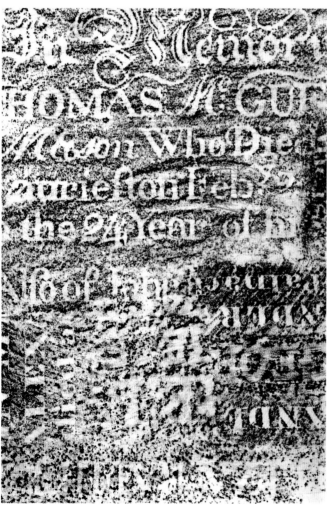

Galloway Hoard project

During the last few years, I have often visited a particularly beautiful location not far from my home. It is an ancient sacred place that has been a religious site for the last 1,000 years. I can see why this is the case: the position is extremely significant in the landscape, elevated above the surrounding fields and almost bordered by the wide River Dee, which winds its way via Loch Ken, down to the sea at Kirkcudbright.

Balmaghie Kirk was built in 1794 and its simple Scottish architecture is striking. I was excited to discover that an archaeological find known as the Galloway Hoard was discovered in an adjoining field in 2014.

The hoard is a unique collection of silver and gold objects from the Viking age in Britain and Ireland. Other unusual items also formed part of the hoard, including glass, rock crystal and pieces of textile and leather.

As an artist I have been very inspired by the combination of this particular landscape, the beautiful building with a fascinating history of its own and the additional magic of a Viking-era discovery at the same site.

I was able to connect all this with my work, when quite by chance I noticed the similarity in appearance between some of my torn strips of rubbings and the patterns on the hacksilver (scrap silver that has been melted down and recast) and arm rings found in the hoard. These were made from narrow strips of silver covered in decorative marks, all quite simply designed but very beautiful.

These creative connections are very exciting when they occur and for the artist it is a question of what to do with them, how to draw all the information together and how to create meaningful pieces of artwork. In my case, it meant I had more reasons to visit the site and also to see the historic exhibition of the hoard, which was shown locally during 2022.

I did some drawings, took photographs, collected leaves and flowers for pressing and took rubbings from one or two of the gravestones that surround the building.

TOP LEFT & RIGHT
Balmaghie Kirk and
surrounding landscape
overlooking the River Dee.

BOTTOM LEFT A wax
crayon rubbing on rice
paper of one of the
gravestones.

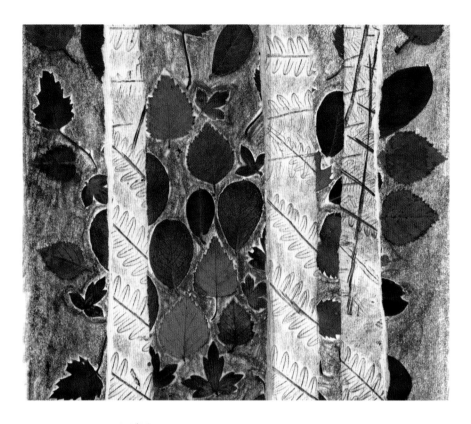

wax + graphite.

Pastel + watercolour.

wax - Pastel watercolour.

Creating a personal response using all this visual information is not an easy process for me. I will have an image in my mind, accompanied by a feeling of confidence, but on the day that I finally sit down to begin the work, it can prove difficult to make progress. What seems so straightforward can turn out not to be the case.

I find the only way through this is to start, make some mistakes, try different experiments, create small examples and be prepared for a kind of visual adventure. This process can be quite lengthy, and things can go in all kinds of directions, but I think if the idea is sound enough, resolution does take place, eventually.

I began by taking rubbings of some of the pressed leaves found at the site. I tore the rubbings into strips and used them as collage material, choosing the best ones with the richest texture. I created a number of samples on small pieces of cartridge paper. I used different materials for the samples, including gouache paint, graphite stick, oil pastels, pressed leaves and rubbings collected from the gravestones (also torn into strips).

TOP LEFT First experiments with rubbings and pressed leaves found in the graveyard.

BOTTOM LEFT Experimenting with colour and texture and introducing the idea of the turquoise verdigris found on some of the silver objects in the hoard.

RIGHT A more spatial piece with some watercolour.

LEFT Small piece using gravestone and pressed leaf rubbings with oil pastel and watercolour (2022). 15 x 20 cm (6 x 8 in)

RIGHT Adding pressed leaves collected from the graveyard (2022). 20 x 30 cm (8 x 12 in)

I moved on to larger-scale pieces using all this information, selecting the colours and textures that were the most suitable. The time spent on this was a very interesting process and has moved my work into new directions, which is essential for me, bringing new ideas and techniques to work with in the future.

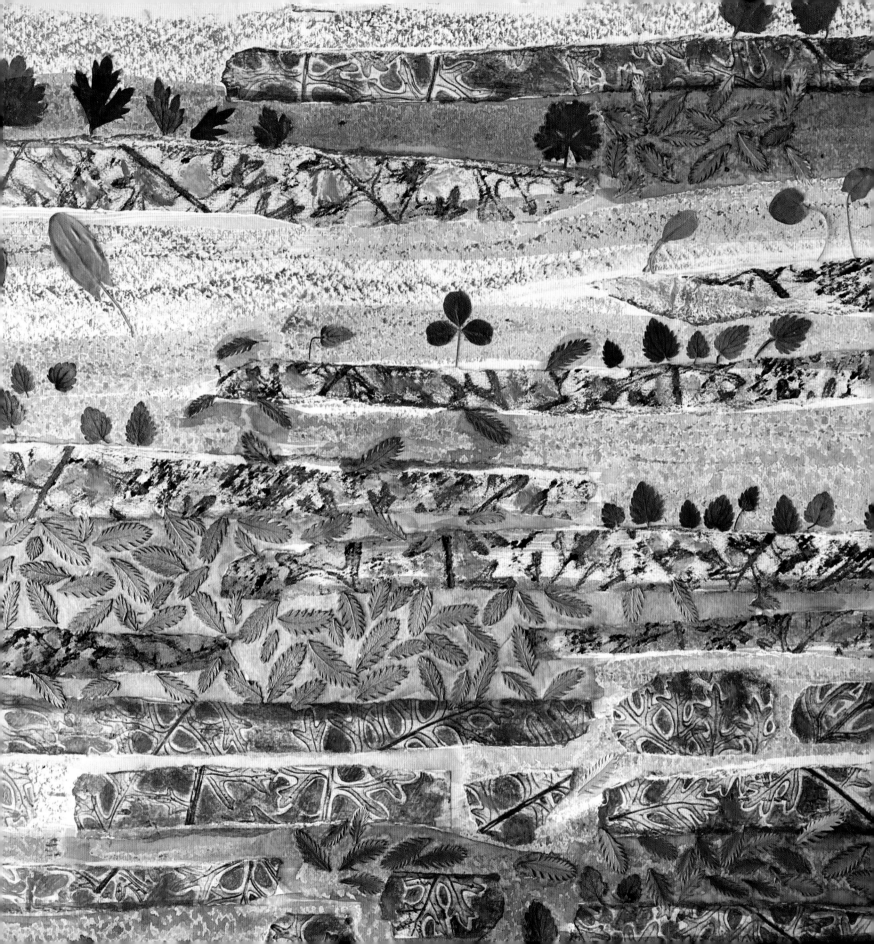

LEFT Using a square background (2022).
40 x 40 cm (16 x 16 in)

RIGHT A larger piece using gravestone and pressed leaf rubbings; pressed leaves and watercolour paint omitting the turquoise wax crayon (2022).
42 x 59 cm (16 ½ x 23 ¼ in)

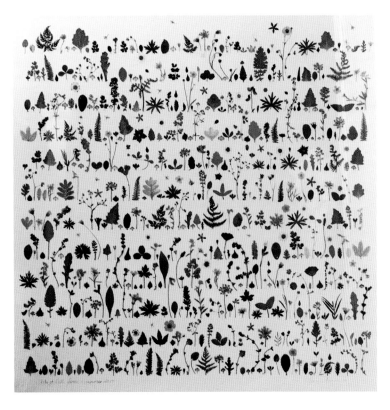

The Isle of Coll, western Scotland

I visited this small south Hebridean island in 2019 and 2021. Here I found the most amazing wild flowers growing in abundance on the machair, a unique habitat found in this part of the world, with a low-lying sandy coastline consisting of shell fragments with sand dunes and cultivated areas for grazing.

It is a very beautiful island and, for me, like another world. The fields are small in scale and protected from intensive farming, principally to encourage the corncrake, a rare bird that lives in undisturbed long grass.

The fields are also full of wild flowers with beautiful colours and textures. The sand dunes also offer another wealth of flora with huge swathes of the bloody cranesbill (*Geranium sanguineum*). The perfume of all these flowers is also notable, a real delight.

The beautiful white sandy beaches provide a different habitat for another group of flora growing in very salty sand and washed by the sea in places. During my first visit in 2019, I managed to collect many samples, collecting small quantities of each plant. I never take very much, a rule I stick to whenever I am collecting.

During the pandemic lockdown I worked on a very large leafwork, which featured most of the material that I collected on the island. This work is now displayed in the community centre in Arinagour on Coll.

My second visit was mainly to deliver the leafwork and to see how things looked at a different time of year. There were still many flowers to be found, the bloody cranesbill was still going strong, and I found some interesting plants growing on the seashore.

Summer

From the Dune
Buzzing bees, red and black moth
Perfume, thyme, clover and bedstraw
Colour, bloody cranesbill, magenta
Bright yellow, trefoil, daisy
Deep bed sphagnum moss
Marram grass holding it altogether
Swallow, light wind
Looking at an empty enormous ocean
Ultramarine

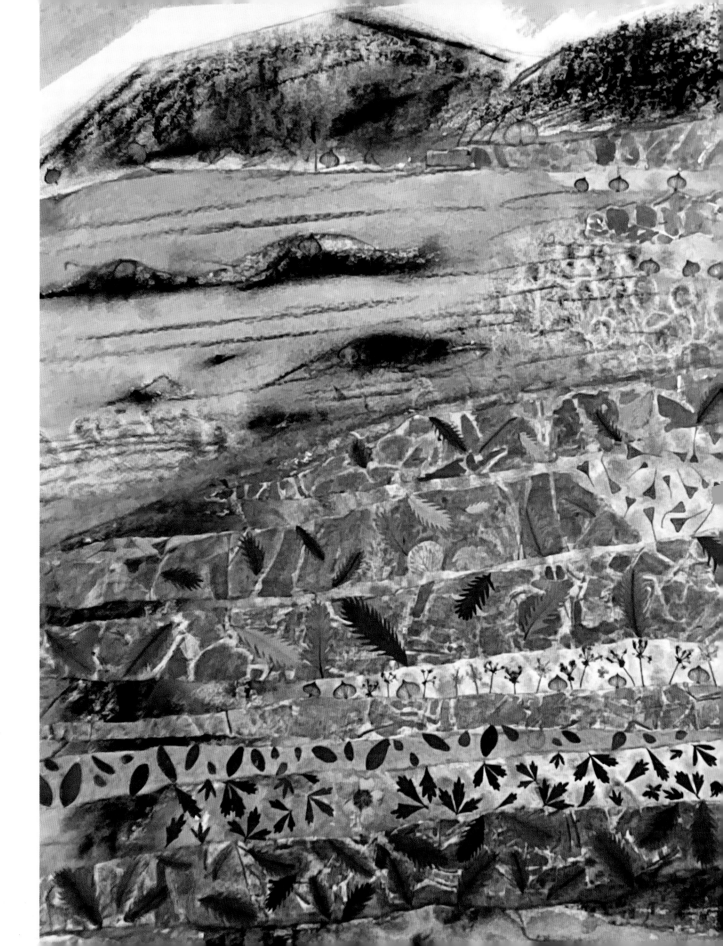

TOP LEFT Isle of Coll flora (2020). 100 x 100 cm (39 x 39 in)

BOTTOM LEFT Small sketch of the coastline of Coll.

RIGHT Finished work combining pressed material from the area, rubbings of pressed leaves and watercolours (2020). 30 x 40 cm (12 x 16 in)

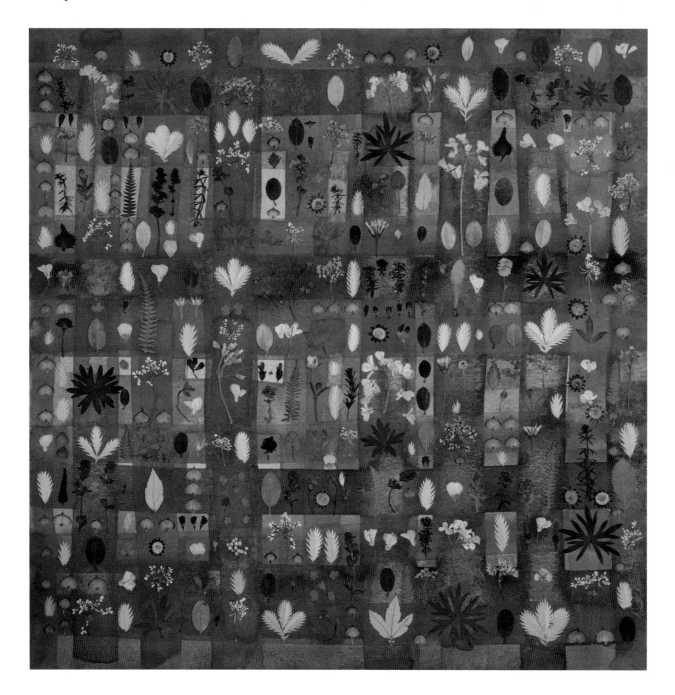

LEFT Finished leafwork using many small pieces of pressed material from my first visit to Coll, on a painted background.

RIGHT Finished leafwork using material collected on my second visit.

Utopia – 'a good place'

This was a title for a piece of work intended to go in a mixed exhibition in 2019, with many artists presenting their interpretation of the title 'Utopia'. My idea was to look at gardens for inspiration, and I arrived at the idea of the Paradise Garden, which is for many people a perfect incarnation of utopia.

The design of this type of garden comes from ancient Persia, where an enclosed and often circular garden was used as a sanctuary for prayer and meditation.

These formal designs were also found in English monasteries, where the apothecary cultivated all the plants needed for healing, and the tradition continues to this day, where herb gardens in particular are designed in a formal, symmetrical style.

With this large exhibition piece, I designed the work from the centre, using my eye and the selection of pressed leaves and flowers I had chosen, with a background colour of grey.

It is possible to draw these formal designs on graph paper or in a sketchbook to work things out before commencing. It is very important to have plenty of material to choose from, especially if the design is symmetrical and the pattern has to be balanced.

Using grey mountboard, 90 × 90 cm (35 × 35in), I placed four squares of iris petals (*Iris* spp.), which retain their deep purple colour. I always use my best colours for a piece like this, especially for the centre of the design.

From there, the formal design was arranged with the centre square edged with triangles of sycamore and finished with dark purple smoke bush leaves (*Cotinus coggygria*), grey raspberry leaves (*Rubus idaeus*), tiny hoheria (*Hoheria* spp.) and London pride flowers (*Saxifraga × urbium*).

Continuing in the formal way, I arranged four squares with one central square of iris and using the same leaves, plus herb robert (*Geranium robertianum*), columbine (*Aquilegia* spp.) and other very small pieces, created a more open arrangement.

I finished the work with four outer squares at the corners, repeating the central square using iris and rose petals with other small pieces.

It is important with a piece of work like this that everything is balanced, which means there has to be plenty of material to choose from to achieve this sort of symmetry.

A second design was achieved in a similar way, with five squares of iris in the centre. The central arrangement was enclosed with a circle of squares, and the design was developed from there, with lots of small pieces arranged in a symmetrical design.

RIGHT *Paradise Garden* (2019). 60 x 60 cm (23 ½ x 23 ½ in)

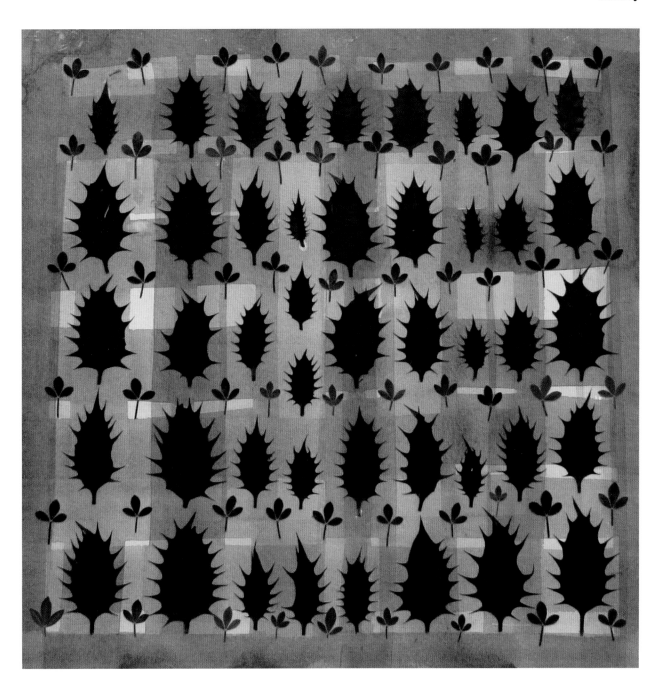

LEFT Foliage collected from a special wood near Sanquhar in south-west Scotland, with a background of a light wash of watercolour (2017). 40 x 40 cm (16 x 16 in)

ABOVE Holly leaves placed on a watercolour background, with a decoration of tiny broom leaves (*Sarothamnus scoparius*) (2019). 25 x 25 cm (10 x 10 in). Small pieces like broom can be used to fill up some of the space between the larger leaves.

LEFT *Hope – A Light in the Darkness* (2019). 60 x 60 cm (23 ½ x 23 ½ in)

RIGHT Silverweed and wild garlic 20 x 20 cm (2021)

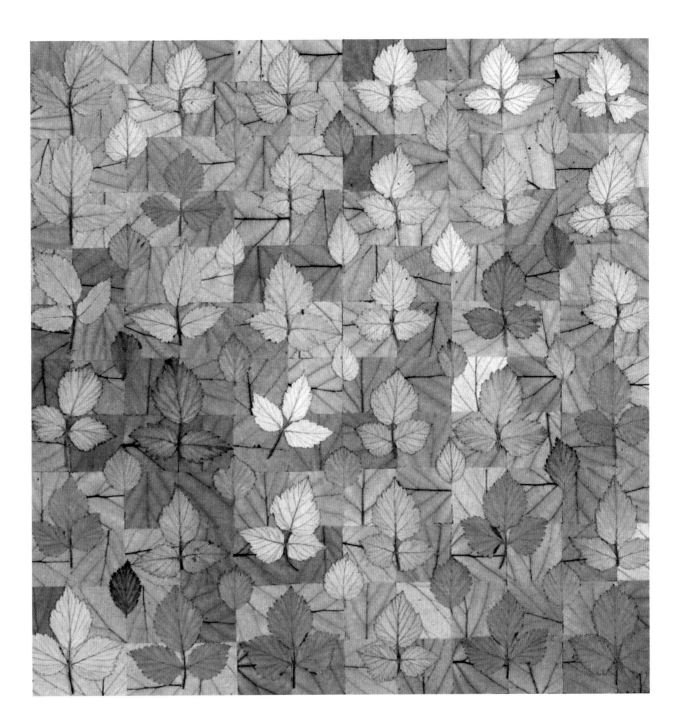

LEFT A variety of small foliage with a few flower petals, including smoke bush leaves (*Cotinus coggygria*), hydrangea petals, ferns and lots of small bits and pieces (2017). 20 x 20 cm (8 x 8 in)

LEFT A finished piece using cut and uncut leaves, all entirely from raspberry (2020). 40 x 40cm (16 x 16 in)

Conclusion

I have enjoyed developing my creative practice during the last few years. I continue to be very open to trying out new ideas and techniques, and I love experimenting. I believe it is important for me to work in this way, constantly looking at new things and refreshing my work. However, I do return to my pressed leaf collection for inspiration and new ideas which come directly from the leaves and flowers themselves, and where they were found.

Leaving Scotland has been a big change which left me feeling a sense of loss and sadness, however the process has been made easier as I moved back to Wales, and another beautiful landscape. My early leafworks of forty years ago were created when I last lived in this area, and I have enjoyed seeing particular trees again like field maples and others in the acer family which grow in abundance.

All the techniques described in this book can be achieved quite easily with little cost. I would encourage readers to start with the looking and collecting process which can be very exciting. Start small with a view of perhaps making leafworks that could be used as greetings cards or as small, framed pictures. Larger pieces could follow which present all kinds of opportunities for designs to appear once the creative process has begun.

Many artists are using the natural world as their creative line of enquiry, investigating natural paints and inks, making charcoal and pastels and papermaking using leaves and flowers amongst other avenues. I believe this highlights our pre-occupation with a more gentle approach to making art and connecting with the natural world in a meaningful way.

RIGHT *Twilight* (2020).
Mixed media, 20 x 30 cm
(12 x 16 in)

Index

Bibliography

Cullen Brown, Joanna, *Let Me Enjoy the Earth: Thomas Hardy and Nature* (W. H. Allen, 1990)

Dean, Jenny, *Wild Colour: How to Make and Use Natural Dyes* (Mitchell Beazley, 2018)

Gifford, Jane, *The Celtic Wisdom of Trees: Mysteries, Magic and Medicine* (Godsfield Press, 2000)

Goldberg, Martin and Mary Davis, *The Galloway Hoard: Viking-age Treasure* (National Museums of Scotland, 2021)

Keble Martin, William, *The Concise British Flora in Colour* (Book Club Associates, 1972)

Know Your Broadleaves (Forestry Commission Booklet, No. 20, 1968)

Lane, John, *The Living Tree: Art and the Sacred* (Green Books, 1988)

Logan, Jason, *Make Ink: A Forager's Guide to Natural Inkmaking* (Abrams NY, 2018)

Mabey, Richard, *Flora Britannica* (Chatto and Windus, 1996)

Mabey, Richard (ed.), with Susan Clifford and Angela King, *Second Nature* (Jonathan Cape, 1984)

William Morris (Victoria and Albert Museum, 1996)

Acknowledgements

I would like to thank Euan Adams for his photography and commitment to this project.

Lizzie Farey, for inspiration and friendship.

Ed and Lucy Campbell, two fellow creative artists full of passion and love of the natural world.

All my fellow artists in Galloway.

Thanks also to my daughter, Amy Parry, for reading and typing the text.

And Batsford for giving me another opportunity to put my creative ideas into book form.

And, as ever, Scotland.